Options Trading

Beginner's Guide to Make Money with Options Trading – All the Strategies to Create an Important Income, in a Short Time

By

Mark Elder, Brian Douglas

professional before attempting any techniques outlined in this book.

By reading this document, the reader agrees that under no circumstances is the author responsible for any losses, direct or indirect, which are incurred as a result of the use of information contained within this document, including, but not limited to, — errors, omissions, or inaccuracies.

Table of Contents

Introduction

Trading the market comes with so many options that you can use; it all depends on your choice and preferences. When you choose certain security, you need to know that it is different from other securities. This book focuses on Options trading and goes ahead to define what it is so that you know what makes it different from other securities on the market.

Options trading is one of the most popular securities that you can trade. This book covers the various concepts of trading as well as what to do to succeed as a new trader. Seasoned traders also have a chance to add to their knowledge when they find aspects of the book that they didn't know before.

The book explores the basics of trading; giving you concepts that get you started. This is a part of a series, meaning you can go for other titles in the book to give you an advanced look at options trading.

Mistakes happen, and when they do, you need to find a solution to these problems. The book explores the different mistakes that happen in trading and look at the solutions that you can explore.

Who is This Book For?

The book is aimed at both novices and seasoned traders alike. Novices can use the book as a stepping stone to advanced techniques, while seasoned traders can use the book as a reference to understand the basics.

Chapter : 1
Options Trading Basics

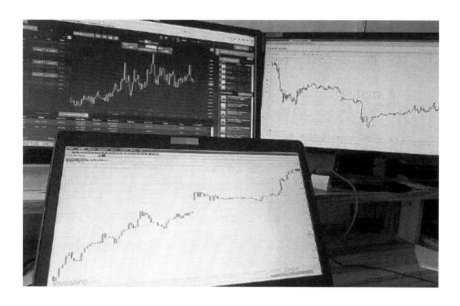

Options trading refers to a contractual agreement between two parties in which the buying party gets the right to trade a security at a predetermined price and at a predetermined date. The right, however, is not obligatory in nature. The right is given to the buyer by the seller through the payment of premiums. Options trading involves trading with stocks and securities for the purpose of profit and also keen to avoid incurring losses. In options trading, the buyer is also referred to as the taker in the contract. The seller is usually referred to as the writer.

Types of Options Trading

There are two types of options trading that grant two different rights. The first one is termed as call options. They give the buyer rights to purchase the asset that is underlying the contract on a later date depending at a predetermined price. This right is, however, not obligatory and is usually based on the discretion of the taker or the contract and his understanding of the market performance in the course of the life of the contract. The life of the contract refers to the period before the contract expires. The price of buying the contract is termed as the exercise price. Sometimes it is also referred to as the strike price.

An example of call options is if Santos Limited has a contract available with shares on security that has the last sale price of $6.00. If the contract has a three-month expiry period, the taker then has the option of offering the shares for a call of $6.00. One can buy 100 token offerings of securities at the said call price per share at the time of choice for the taker in the course of the life of the contract. The taker is also required to pay premiums to the writer of the contract for the option. To fully own the call rights, one has to exercise it based on the predetermined dates that are specified in the agreement.

Options Trading

On the hand, the writer of the contract has an obligation to ensure that the shares that are purchased are delivered. In the above example, the writer has to deliver 100 security token offerings as long as the taker of the contract has exercised the option. However, the writer sustains reception of option premium during the life of the contract regardless of Put whether or not the taker exercises the option.

The other form of options is the put options. These ones are designed to grant the taker rights of selling the underlying assets for a price that has been predetermined by the contract. The rights to sell have to be exercised in the course of the life of the contract. Just like the call options, the taker of the contract is not compelled to exercise the right. In this case, the buyer only provides the shares required in the agreement if the put right is exercised.

An example of a put option is when a contract by the writer has a predetermined $6.00 put token offering for a predetermined period of three months. The taker has a put option of selling 100 security token offerings as shares at the said price of $6.00 per share. This sell right has to be exercised in eth active life of the contract by the date of expiry of the agreement.

As with the call option, the taker still has to pay premiums to the writer for the contract and the trade to be valid. The right is only valid when it is exercised with the course of the life of the contract. Outside of it, the right is forfeited regardless of whether or not value was created out of the contract. This means that the taker of the contract has to be keen on market performance and judge well whether or not to invoke the sell rights and when. Sometimes, a taker will opt not to exercise the right of sale of shares as the contract expiry dies out.

The exercise style is usually dependent on the system used. Two systems are usually used: the American style and the European style. The European style usually compels the taker to exercise the right in the contract only on the expiry date. The American style is more flexible and allows the exercise of the right any time before the date of expiry of the agreement.

Advantages of Option Trading

Option trading has many advantages for investors. Essentially, it is an investment that offers an opportunity for those who have the capital to delve into an income generation venture. Advantages with options trading are multiple and should motivate people into the sector of trading securities, selling and buying assets as well as earning interests that accrue.

Options Trading

First is the ability of this venture to aid to manage risks when investing in stocks and securities. They can cushion one from having to incur losses in investment. This is because investing in the stocks and shares usually involves risks of all in the value of the shares. This devaluation can lead to a dwindling of the profits and may, in fact, cut into the shares that one holds. However, the options marketing ensure that one is hedged from such uncertainty and as well as guarantees that a person can earn value from the trading of the shares.

Options trading is also advantageous is it allows someone the time to decide about purchase or not. This is particularly the advantage of the call options. The contract usually has a period during which a person considers the exercise of the implied rights. The person studies the market and its performance and has the allowance to understand his financial situation before making a decision on whether to purchase the shares or not. This leads one to make decisions about investments that are reasoned out. It always comes with more preparedness to handle the consequences of the decisions that one takes. This helps to rid the habit of making trading decisions on whims that can later lead to anxiety and worry as market forces swing into play.

The freedom of action to exercise an option is also an exciting aspect of trading. This is because this is a speculative filed based on eth analysis of market forces and performance. Once one enters an option contract, they can happily enjoy trading them without the obligation to exercise the rights included in the contract. One can, in fact, just understand the market landscape and opt for a trade investment with an option that one does not even have intentions of exercising. On the speculative conception of options trading, one can decide to just exercise the purchase right in a call option when they know the market environment is getting better and promises value. They can also decide to exercise the sell option when losses are expected to avoid the loss or salvage a profit margin.

Leverage

Leverage is a very advantageous aspect of options trading that people try to take advantage of and participate in the security market. In leverage, one has to place smaller outlays with a prospect of making higher profits in view. This encourages those who do not have the capital to invest in the underlying assets or shares to find a way of investing and get returns. One of the important parts of leverage is that one is usually getting back returns from the underlying assets or shares, yet they have not been required to pay the full cost for the purchase of the shares.

In the idea of leverage also is also the advantage of diversification. This by creating a portfolio without incurring huge initial outlays. This diversification can then create a stream of investment channels that in practice, lead to profits increasing one's earnings. Sometimes this income can increase to go above one's dividends when one takes call options that are laid again the shares owned. This extra income can even emanate from the shares that are integrated having been acquired from a lending facility. Option premiums also come ahead of the trading activities and hence cushioning one from any chances of loss.

Components of an Option Contract

There are various standardized components of option contracting that enable ease in engaging in options trading. These components characterize the mechanics of how options trading binds the parties involved and demonstrates the ay profits can be generated if the market forces are favorable. Among the components of options trading are:

- Underlying securities

- Contract size

- Expiry day

- Exercise prices

Underlying securities

Options that are traded on the market only apply to certain assets. These assets are then referred to as underlying securities. The word shares can be replaced with the word shares in certain instances. There are companies that provide the asset against which the option operators list options. ASX is one operator in the options trading market has played a key role in the listing of underlying securities.

The term classes of options refer to the listing of puts and calls as options of the same assets. As an example, is when puts and calls are applied to a lease corporation's shares. This does not put in regard the contract terms in terms of the predetermined price or duration of expiry of the call and put contracts. An operator of options trading usually provides the list of the available classes for the benefit of investors.

Contract Size

On the ASX platform of options trading, the market standardizes the size of the option contract at 100 underlying securities. One option contract, therefore, corresponds to 100 underlying shares. The changes that can happen only come when reorganization happens on the initial outlay of the underlying share or the capital therein. Index options usually fix the value of the contract at a certain stipulated dollar rate.

Expiry day

Options are constrained by time and have a life span. There are predetermined expiry deadlines that the platform operator sets which have to be respected. These deadlines are usually rigid, and once they are out the rights under a contract in a particular class of unexercised options are then forfeited. Usually, the last day of the life span of a contract is the summative trading date. For shares that have their expiry coming by June of 2020, the options over them have their last trading day on a Thursday that comes before the last Friday that happens to be in the month. Those that expire beyond June 2020, expiry is on the third Thursday that happens to be in the month. For index options. Expiries come on the concurrent third Thursday of the same month of writing the option. However, these dates can be readjusted by the options platform operator as and when there is a reason for such action.

In recent years, platform operators have introduced more short-term options for some underlying. Some are weekly, while others are on a fortnightly basis. These ones have the corresponding weekly or fortnightly expiries. When the life span of options run out, the operators then create new deadlines. However, all classes of options have their expiries subject to quarters of the financial calendar.

11

Exercise Prices

These are the buying price or the price of selling the assets or underlying securities. These prices are also called strike prices. They are usually predetermined in the option contract and have to be met if one has to exercise the rights in an option. Essentially, they are called exercise because the parties are now invoking the rights that are stipulated in an option either to buy or sell. The exercise of the option is, therefore, subject to the price stipulations.

The prices are usually predetermined by the platform operator. Various prices can be listed as available on the market for the same expiry of a certain class of options. Usually, prices depend on the value of the underlying share value. If the value of the underlying prices increases, the exercise prices also increase commensurately. The need to offer a range of prices for the same option contract is in order to suit the market conveniences of buyers of the contracts. The buyer can better match their own expectations of the pricing of the underlying shares in view of the position of their option contract. The exercise prices can also be varied in the course of an active contract when market dynamics dictate that such a move has to be made.

Premium

This is the value of the option that is usually expressed as a price that has to be paid by the option taker. Of the five features of options trading, this is the only one that is not determined by the platform operator. Usually, the premium prices are stated in cents corresponding to the value per share. To get the premium that has to be paid, for an option that is of relatively standard size, a formula is set. One has to take the premium price that has been stipulated on the option contract and multiply by the sum of the shares that a contract has.

For example, when the cost of a premium has been quoted as 16 cents. This has to be multiplied by the standard shares for every option, which is 100. This brings the payable premium for the option to $16.00. For an index option, there is another formula that offers a modality of calculating the premium. Index options have a standard multiplier index of $10. The quoted premium is therefore multiplied by this index multiplier to result to the total payable premium.

Having exercised the rights under an option contract, there are guidelines with regard to being eligible to vote and to earn dividends from the shares. The buyer in the case of a call option does not gain express rights to earn dividends on the shares. One has to wait until the exercised right of purchase is affected by the transfer of the shares. The same applies to vote rights. Usually, shares represent a voice in the company invested in. however; the voting rights also wait or the transfer of the shares to the buyer.

Similarly, the seller or writer in the put option does not expressly acquire the right to vote and earn dividends. One waits until the underlying assets, securities, or shares are transferred. This helps to create a structure of transfer of shareholding and transfer of the same. Any disputes about the expired contract have to be resolved, and proper registration of buying and selling be done for the holding trading the shares or asset.

Adjustments to Option Contracts

There is a general effort to ensure that option contracts are entered in under conditions that are standardized to the greatest extent possible. However, some market forces may upset the set optimum conditions and specifications. This may call or the making of some adjustments for the purpose of ensuring the preservation of the value attached to the positions of the various options contracts that have been entered into by various takers and writers.

In making the adjustments, it has to be established the kind of upset that has been caused on the market. Usually, it may affect one or more components of the options market. Identifying the affected components is necessary so that the adjustment is specific and particular to the kind of area of trading affected.

ASX, as one of the platform operators, has its rules that try to retain a tentatively predictable and standardized environment of trade. However, it also provides guidelines for the kind of measures that have to be made when adjustments are required. Conventions that guide the process of adjustment cushion participants on this kind of market and also protect takers and writers from arbitrary actions that may be unfavorable.

Options Pricing Fundamentals

When one is considering participating in options trading, certain aspects of this market are fundamental to consider. One is the premium and how it is calculated. This has been discussed earlier under the components of options trading. However, option premiums usually vary based on different factors that may affect them directly. The most important is the value of the share that underlies the particular option. The remainder of the time before the option also times out is also a determining. Option premium has two parts that comprise its total value. Intrinsic value is the first part and is followed by the time value.

Intrinsic value

This is the value as a result of calculating the difference between the exercise price that is quoted for a certain option trade and the market value the underlying asset over which options trading has been applied. This calculation should be a constant and be valid at any time of the life span of the contract. This will expose the motivation behind entering an options contract for the particular option. The intrinsic value of an option is usually important since it does not vary much and is not impacted upon by market forces or other external factors.

Time Value

This refers to the pressure that time exerts on a particular option as the life span progresses. It is important to analyze the market forces for the mere reason that times may get better to lead to an increase in the value of the option in the course of the period before the expiry of the option. One, therefore, has to be willing to pay to ensure that one takes advantage of an option whose value has gone high in the course of time.

Usually, there is a period when an option is at its most profitable stage. This is the time when one should consider buying the option and hence should always prepare for this time. Some options that do not have high intrinsic value may also have high time value if they are subject to market forces.

However, they also pose a high risk of losses. The rate of decay of time value is not constant and may not be calculated mathematically. However, the rate of decay accelerates towards the end of the life span of the option.

Chapter : 2
How to Start Options Trading

Appreciate That Options Trading Is Not Simple

It is vital at this stage to recapitulate the meaning of options trading. This is a contract that grants one the right of either buying or selling a security based on the speculative value of it in a limited period of time. However, the contract is not obligatory in nature. In understanding options trading, two forms of it have to be understood; first is a call option, and the other is the put option. The two are opposites of each other. One buys the former option when one expects an asset's value to go up over time but before the deadline of expiry of the contract expires. This allows one to buy an asset at a relatively lower price. The latter is the opposite entailing buying the right to exercise sell of an asset if one speculates that price of the asset would go down in the period before the expiry of the contract.

However, participating in this market requires one to have enough understanding of how it works. Any venture requires one to learn enough. Educating oneself generally about investment is the best standing point. This creates understanding and ensures that one is able to comprehend the way that the options trading market as an investment venture works.

Among the reasons why people should educate themselves on options trading is because it does not work in certain ways. It also does not have guarantees of profit. This means that it, just like other ventures, involves risks that should be understood. The risks in the case of trading options are quite extreme. It requires calculation and being accurate as one speculates about the drop and rising of the value of the options on offer. Being interest in a venture that involves a high-risk level requires enough knowledge and sometimes mentorship by those who have prior knowledge and understanding of the market in order to avoid plunging into frustration and wastage of capital.

One of the motivating aspects of trading options is that it allows one to capitalize on the advantage of leverage. Leverage is the means by which one can use the low capital investment to guarantee profits; all is not sweet and sugar. Essentially, options have underlying assets of greater value that it controls. However, one can edge into the potential purchase of this asset or acquisition of the underlying shares and the advantages that it comes with at a relatively affordable rate. However, the period for capitalizing the leverage is limited as there is a predetermined date, and the life span of the rights that have to be exercised expire. This may lead to losses.

In understanding options trading, the exact manner of risk has to be clear to one. The purchase of options is speculative, and this can be done as a cushion against incurring losses. When traders are able to make speculative purchases, it sets them up to potentially making huge returns. However, this is a gamble as one has to be accurate with the way they comprehend and predict the market forces, patterns, and trends. Predictions have to be accurate about the magnitude, the timing, and influences that impact on the price and value of the underlying asset. However, it puts the traders liable to potentially huge losses and has to content with incurring trade commissions that are usually quite high. Novice traders should get it right that options trading is more or less like a gamble, and risks are invaluable high. However, they are not prohibitively high as some have ventured into this market and have found some good level of success.

However, the options have been used, as opposed to making huge returns in profit, to protect people's stock investments. This is particularly the case with the put option that entails one putting one's shares up for sale in fear of an imminent drop of the share prices on the market. This way of using options has turned out safer and better in cushioning people against losses since one only forfeits the price of the contract.

Read and Understand Essential Literature Available On Options Trading

Reading is part of the process of educating one's self in business. A lot of literature is currently available on various platforms for the benefit of those seeking to understand investments and avenues of investment. Success and failure stories are also hugely available, particularly on the internet where people could acquire first-hand accounts on the options trading venture.

However, reading is only helpful if the correct material is being read. Not every account of business success stories is true. Some are exaggerated while others are written to arouse interest to influence people into making certain decisions for business purposes. The internet is full of hidden business activities, some of which are even hidden behind the sensational headlines of the literature resources striking people's eyes on their phones and computers. This means that knowledge is only good when it comes from the correct source.

There is a booklet that has reliable and valid information for those seeking understanding. It is entitled "Characteristics and Risks of Standardized Options."

This book is a comprehensive detail of just about everything that needs to be known about options trading. It is not written for other interest other than to expose the real mechanics of the trading and how it functions particularly at its most complicated level. It complies with the regulations of SEC, and it is usually distributed by the firms that operate in brokerage in this sector. It is usually issued to those who express interest to participate in trading by opening accounts for options trading. In the booklet, there is a better exposition of the concepts that apply in this industry and as well list the various available options trade classes that one could try out.

It also explains concepts of exercising spelling out how the taxman relates with options trading for the purpose of comprehension of the entire options-trade venture. It also considers the associated risks to ensure that readers are beware of the venture they are setting themselves up to join. If one has an interest in options trading, this is a must have read as one remains vigilant about some wrong information particularly by dubious brokers and businessmen who may mislead with an inaccurate representation of the trade.

Acquire an Understanding of the Basics of the Kinds of Trades

The kinds of trades have been discussed already. The trades are basically either a call option or the put option. These have to be understood well since they are the start of knowing this trade as an investment. The types of trade are the core part of the knowledge that a person can gain on options trading. All these can be explained with a desire to gain an understanding of how each of the two types of trades works. This can be achieved the desire for understanding can involve seeking mentorship or seeking consultancy firm. It can call for some level of schooling in order to begin to attain literacy, especially for those people who did not have prior knowledge of economic investments.

Having understood some of the concepts, one should internalize them. This is by reflecting on what has been learned so far about options trading and starting to view oneself as a potential expert who can even teach others. The way to do this is by, for instance, examining oneself on the understanding of the concepts. Some consultants have advised beginners to create a spreadsheet containing the various concepts and terms that are of the essence in understanding options trading. The terminologies have to be clearly stated in a way that does not obscure meaning.

Some of the important terms have already been explained in the initial chapter. However, the following terms are still vital in the understanding of option trading;

- Holder refers to a person who purchases an options trade.
- Writer is a term for the seller of the options trade.

Strike price that is also referred to as the exercise price is the amount that has to be paid for the purchase or sale of a security – in this case depending on whether the trade is of the call or put type. A stick needs to go above or below the strike price, depending on the option type, in order for a profit to be registered on the purchased option.

Date of expiry is the deadline by which the rights in an option have to be exercised to either buy or sell share or the underlying security. After this date, the rights contained in the options trade are lost.

"In the money' is a term employed to indicate whether a market price, as compared to the strike price, is lower or higher. This helps to indicate whether the option is a call or put when it is higher than it is a call, and it is a put when "in the money" is lower.

"Out of the money" is the same concept as "in the money" only that it denotes the converse. It shows that in the case of a call, the underlying asset's market price is lower as compared to the exercise price. In the case of a put, "out of the money" refers to a state where the market price is higher as compared to the strike price. This means that "out of the money" implies a loss while "in the money" implies a profit.

These terms are, therefore, a vital part of understanding options trading. As it is, this trade has its own jargon and can, on the outset appear unattractive. The complexity of it is only represented by the appearance of the language that describes it. For people who may not be so much interested in options trading, they get exhausted right at the stage of hearing these terms. Extra efforts have to be made to develop a body of knowledge first in order to forge a path to understanding.

Brokerage Account

Having understood how the trade works, it becomes essential to set up a brokerage where one can start creating a portfolio of transactions. As with anything about this venture, one has to know what it is they are going for when opening an account for brokerage. This is in order to ensure that nothing happens in the process of setting up an account that can later cause regret. Sometimes failures in investment can be traced back to just a single mistake along the way.

By understanding everything in opening a brokerage, one has to consider various factors that have an influence on the trade. First is to mind about the commissions that brokerages impose on the trading of various types of options. This is because it is an investment and one have to scout for the best deal that does not deal so much of expenses that impede value generation.

When one does not have the requisite knowledge on what the commission rates signify, it is based to seek interpretations. A brokerage should not obscure one from what is going on with the option trade. One has to be able to attain conversance with everything in the industry and ensure that he is able to seek all clarifications. As a matter of fact, one has to go in and research on the track record of the brokerages in order to shortlist those that are likely to best suit one's conveniences and trade interests.

One has to be alert for scammers and brokerages that are likely to give a raw deal. Some may want to take advantage of the ignorance and lack of technical knowledge of trading to exploit unsuspecting buyers and sellers. It is, in fact, necessary that trust is based less on persuasion and more the track record of the brokerage. It should be reputable, and a referred one is better. Only after thorough research is concluded and all reservations allayed that one should take a step to make any money transfers or deposits. Any brokerage with reported negative reviews and complaints of fraud should be avoided by all means.

In order to start trading options, it requires one to secure approval of the brokerage. Approvals depend on certain standards of merit. Some set thresholds of deposits in a brokerage account in order to give approval. The experience of the holder is also considered in order to ensure that those who are approved to start buying and selling know exactly what they are doing. Covered calls cannot be written if there is no account for options trading exists. Additionally, brokerages houses want to be sure that the risks that are related to the sector are well understood in order to give the green light to proceed.

Comprehending Technical Analysis

Options are usually limited by time due to the expiry date that is one of the conditions inhering this type of trading. They are, hence, short-term and have a life span. This means one is analyzing how prices for the underlying asset are behaving on the market with the intention to know when to exercise the rights in a bought option. This is for the purpose of ensuring that a profit margin is secured by all means possible. It is also to ensure that a healthy return on the invested capital through the purchase of an option is guaranteed. However, understanding the mechanics of price variations on the market in light of the desired profit margin that one is targeting one has to learn about technical analysis.

One has to educate themselves about the steadiness of market performance. Support and resistance levels of the market are to be studied in view of this. This is with regard to the level of performance that is relatively optimum on the market and which stock usually can neither go beyond or below. The lowest point is the support level, while the highest level is the resistance level. Usually, the support level is understood by studying historical trends of purchase to identify the level at which most purchases of an asset were purchased over time. The resistance level points at the value levels expressed as price, at which high sales of an asset or underlying security registered over time.

It is also vital to appreciate the significance of volume on the patterns of trading and price movements. In this regard, it refers to the movement of a stock in a certain direction of market performance that may be an indicator of profitability. This can be read as an opportunity to exercise rights or otherwise the "in the money" phenomenon. However, this is usually speculative, and accuracy depends on the experience and level of expertise in technical analysis of the options-trading forces.

It is also vital to be able to study chart patterns and make sense of them. Usually, these are based on the cliché that history repeats itself. Certain environmental phenomena usually result in predictable market response. High investment levels in the country, for instance, is an indicator of better stock price performance. Tax policies and how they are reviewed also relate to corresponding market behavior that may have been experienced from the past. This being said, it means that someone has to develop a love for studying graphs and going into historical economics in order to boost the development of intuition of reading trends that are telling of market performance.

Moving averages also are part of the knowledge that has to be learned in the interest of boosting technical analysis abilities. These averages usually are watched as they are the triggers of hope or doom. They are predictors of how the market will also behave either constantly or if there will be a lot of variations in the behavior of the market. Making sense of these also comes with experience in the trading industry in order to relate what they indicate. Once this has been learned, it will be easier to detect signals that determine decisions that have to be made with regard to the purchase of options.

Start Slow by Making Trials

In starting paper trading, one sets off by "paper trading." This is avoiding the habit of throwing caution at the wind and assuming that one has learned enough about the trade to start risking. Options trading requires one only to commit risk money that one is likely not to be hurt badly if they lose. One cannot commit money that they have labored much to earn to a venture whose technique of trade one has just learned. Paper trading requires one to test the waters with one leg by practicing and seeing how things go. One has to start slow, worrying out with little for a period of some months before they can really judge if they are acquiring the required experience and knowledge to handle the trading.

There is a way even to pretend. This can be done through software meant for practicing traders. Returns have to be observed for a streak of a few months, and when realized that the trend is returning well, one can then start to plunge into actual options trading gradually. The advantage of paper trading is that it is some form of fooling around that is done objectively for the purpose of seasoning and familiarization. It does not have the psychological weight that would otherwise be felt with actual trading when one is just starting trading. It helps to learn how trading works, to correlate the factors that influence the trading, and to enable one put into practice some of the knowledge gained while educating oneself about options trading.

Even in the trials, one has to try to be calculative with the capital to plow in. As already stated, this is a highly risky venture, and a learner cannot fully bear taking losses that he cannot understand how they were incurred. One should also adopt limit orders; this is by not purchasing options at their market prices since the price of executing them may turn out to be higher than one had anticipated. One has to determine how much they want to purchase options in order to capitalize on leverage.

Chapter : 3
Platforms and Tools for Options Trading

A vital aspect of options trading is the platform that one uses to trade. This is because options trading requires monitoring and requires a continuous analysis of trends. Performance is also monitored, and since the trade is impacted upon by a complex of factors, one has to choose a suitable platform for trading.

A good platform for trading should offer a lot of opportunities for traders. These are opportunities to orient beginners into trading, development for the existing ones, and actualization for those with a record on the platform. A platform of trading should also prescribe the available products and any resources that subscribers on the platform can benefit from to push themselves to profitability.

With the technology developing at high speed, platforms continue to improve by the day. This is both complicating the trading itself as well as providing avenues of spreading awareness about the business. A platform should, therefore, have the ability to offer the best possible experience for the traders to do trade and grow both in experience and returns without meeting a lot of platform limitations and frustrations.

A Platform Takes Trading To the Holders

Trading involves a lot of complexities that may sometimes be scary. It makes people lose interest as soon as they develop it. They perceive it as too complicated. The impression is that it is a venture meant for the people who have higher comprehension of concepts in the economics specialty and that those who do not a background in this area will have difficulty getting on board.

However, a trading platform has to present options trading as a venture that is possible and in which anyone with interest can succeed in. The days when options trading and any other forms of trading were presented as a show of sophistication are long gone. In this era, every sector of investment is being portrayed as possible, and businesses are now being made easier in order to create a better chance for people to dare. A platform that limits investment so much and is exclusive in terms of how it carries out its trading activities is irrelevant to modern economic patterns.

Platforms, therefore, have to be interactive and user-friendly. They should have the ability to encourage users to feel like they can handle the trade. It should also have the capability to gauge the level of use and give feedback about how well they are able to use it. If it is a website, for instance, it has to be able to report the numbers as people visit it and how many eventually end up creating accounts and trading. Counting traffic is essential for feedback that can lead to the creation of a better experience for the users.

Competition

The reason for considering a good platform is because the competition is high today. Competition has led to the creation of better trading experiences through innovation. Platforms are now trying to out-do each other in being the avenues of options trading. They are doing this by striving to create ways of improving user experience. It is therefore essential to identify the various parameters of comparing the platforms.

Eventually, one has to choose a platform that offers optimal access to the trading world.

In choosing a platform sometimes, one would want to take advantage of the advantages of different platforms. This is looking at one's style of trading and how they wish to monitor their business and see if a platform is more transparent in handling the tares or whether it offers a clear lens of controlling purchases and sells of options. This is the reason why the various platforms have to be assessed in terms of their potential. Usually, platforms are related to the tools of trading. Some of the tools of trading can be found right on the platform of trading.

When a platform of trading also has various tools of aiding trading, it ensures that one can gain a lot of benefits at one place. This makes the platform a utility platform where a person can visit for more purposes than just trading. It also makes it better. For instance, if a platform has videos that offer trading tutorials. This can make it resourceful in imparting competency in participating in the very sector that the platform operates.

To best benefit from competition, one has to understand the type of trade they want to do. This is by naming their price and gauging which platform can serve better in ensuring returns and value generation. This is in order to avoid going into trading in desperation, and one has to be patient to see if the platform can also come out and meet a trader at their point of ability and also help in trading in comfort where risk is at a minimum.

Types of Trading Platforms

There are various platforms in options trading that one could consider. There is web-based trading that utilizes the power of the search engines. This platform has many operators since the building of websites in the modern age is easy. This platform is responsible for the growth in the popularity of options trading. People can trade from anyone, open brokerage accounts, make deposits, and participate in the buying and selling of assets in the comfort of their homes.

With the presence of a lot of technological gadgets such as smartphones, tablets, and computers, web-based trading has been easy and possible. Websites can be built with additional resources for learning and tools that can be an advantage for both novice and seasoned traders. On the websites, regular updates on the market can be posted to keep traders informed about trends, patterns, and even help in analyzing price movements for the subscribers.

The web is also a good platform when it comes to filtering opportunities and options based on suitability and preference in view of the various abilities of users. They can be designed to be customizable even when the options markets are standardized.

User Friendliness

Usually, websites are good as they offer various tools that aid beginners to edge into trading options. ASX, for example, offers a variety of web-based resources that guide people in their efforts to understand trading. This includes online chats that have instant feedback as a team is dedicated to the work site for correspondence purposes. The aim of this is to offer motivation and impetus to go on with the discovery of the markets trends until one becomes a seasoned trader.

Friendliness is also in terms of the efforts that are made to create peer assistance. This is through creating groups of traders that influence each other and can learn from the vast experiences in the trading of the options. This can be a positive influence on the journey to gaining competence and help support an environment where people can relate and interact as they pursue their various financial goals.

It is important to consider the fact that some of the platforms of trading offer important tools that can be helpful in deciding on options. The tools are those that help in monitoring markets and simplify the technical analysis process for the trader. This can help one to sharpen their trading strategy to align well with the ultimate goal of trading. This depends on whether the goal of trading is to earn money in terms of profit or hedge oneself against losses on the underlying asset.

Tools to Learn

Upon mastering the various basics of trading and making the initial moves to start trading, one has to use various tools that help to indicate the advancers and decliners on the market. Greeks are some kind of metrics that those involved in options trading capitalize to ensure maximization of returns. These "Greeks" include the delta matrix that measures the correlation between price movements of the underlying asset relative to the price of the option. The tools for monitoring the movements for these parameters of trading are vital as everyone is always trading with a focus on minimizing losses while geared towards profit maximization.

The gamma is another tool that can help to predict market trends in order to do good timing for decisions on exercising rights in options. Gamma is an indicator of the rate of delta variations for the option price as compared to the asset price. This goes hand in hand with the time-decay tool that indicators the value movement, either upwards or downwards, in the period of life options. This helps to signal which options to avoid given the remaining time of the life span and the value implications thereon.

There is also the aspect of the volatility of the asset underlying a particular option trade. Some of the assets or stocks do not have inherent volatility to appreciate in value due to their nature. Assets that have high market volatility usually gain a lot on the market, and hence, the value behaves better to favor the call option trade. Products with ugh volatility and high inherent value are not suitable for the put option trade since they will occasion a loss. It is therefore important to use correct tools that aid in the analysis if the technical mechanics of the options trading business.

Tools are not just concrete things that can be manipulated. Some tools, especially in trading, are conceptual in nature. This is because they are the ones by which one can trade and aid in decision making. They sample out market forces and help in mapping out market trends for the benefit of the trader. To perceive tools as only concrete in nature is a misconception of the whole options trading venture.

Professional level platforms

There is a level in trading where one attains sophistication and attains the intuition to thrive in options trading regardless of the ways market forces seem to behave. At this level, someone needs tools that can help them edge into the horizon of complexity in trading. The platforms for this professional level exist, and they have to offer tools that are an edge above the basic level. These tools have to offer strategies of competing to control the stocks and rise above the market forces. At this level, one becomes daring, and the possibilities that the platform offers should only be dared by those who have mastered trading and are sure of beating odds as they speculate about squeezing out value form trades that otherwise be perceived as highly risky.

The platform should be full of idea probing resources that lead one to gain the courage to trade more and more. Web-based platforms of this level include the think or swim platform that is categorically for seasoned traders. This is the reason why one has to know the platform to trade on based on their level of experience in options trading. Some platforms are too complicated for the starters. The tools are even out of the capacity of a beginner to comprehend the trades appear to have higher risks that may wipe away hard-earned fortunes.

Mobile Trading

Some platforms have taken advantage of the handiness of the mobile era. These entail the smartphone lifestyle and the flashier iPod, iPad, and tablet culture. This is when trading is being placed in the palms of traders to hold and run away with it. This platform usually targets traders that want to capitalize on device optimization. This is the reason why trades have classes. Some of the options could be device targeted as they can only be taken advantage of when one using the suitable device for trading, provided the relevant support tools that the device offers.

Mobile trading also comes in order to keep people abreast. This is because opportunities sometimes appear and disappear on people because they are not using a device that enables them to be precise and timely in decision making and action.

With mobile trading, apps have been developed, some with notification capability. One can customize the apps to ensure that no opportunity comes that is not taken advantage of. Opportunities' in trading have to be seized and relying on a platform that is less handy and far means that opportunities of trading are lost.

What Are We Looking For In Platforms And Tools?

First is the opportunity to learn. There is no worse platform of trading than that which targets only to admit traders who do not understand what they are getting into. The education that a platform has to offer should be free as trading is itself risky enough to prohibit any extra expenses in the process. Platform operators should understand that any interested person who visits their platform is a potential subscriber, and they should freely offer support to educate them for the purpose of acquisition of requisite knowledge on options trading.

Some of the platforms have gone as opening structures units for education on options trading. These courses are taken online, and coaching is done through the provision of a stream of webinars transmitted live or uploading recorded ones. This is for platforms that appreciate that trading is an informed gamble that requires one to know enough. They even test the proficiency of understanding trading concepts and mechanics for the purpose of ensuring that any people who trade on the platform are doing what they understand to build the platform ratings.

It is also vital for a starter to set standards that the broker's customer service should pass. In trading, brokers should work enough to earn the commission that they charge on the options that subscribers trade on buy. This is because some brokers are obscure and may not involve the options trader who is buying options in decisions that directly impact on his capital. One, therefore, faces a lot of anxiety if the broker is not responsive and transparent on the particular mechanics that influence trade.

Excellent broker services try to suit customer needs. They ask options traders subscribed to their platform what their preferred means of reaching is. Whether a live chat or phone call suits the customer or not. They also dedicate a desk for trading communications and queries and has the discipline to listen to customers and their issues with patience. They, in fact, have feedback on the quality of customer service that those who reach out get.

Software Trading Platforms

These are more complex than web-based ones. This is because they are run on the trader's computer, and the trader is required to understand what the software does and interpret it. Even when the brokerage can offer assistance, software-based platforms require the trader to have enough technical know how to read charts, graphs, and understand patterns that represent various components of options trading.

For beginners, a complex platform has to be avoided by all means. This is because one is bound to engage in aspects of trading that they do not have an understanding of. A trading platform simply has to be simple and clear. The interface should not be too busy as to scare away those traders who are not accustomed. This is the reason why operators usually separate the platforms that as designed for basic use, which is suitable for novices, and advanced trading for the seasoned ones.

Then a broker has to offer a tutorial that guides the user on how to navigate their platform. Everything has to be explained, even those that one would deem to be obvious. Screenshots can even be available in order to be categorical and emphatic. This ensures that a broker has offered all possible assists for the trader to benefit from the offers and products on the platform successfully.

Cost Implication

It is important for the trader to know that some brokers may have charges attached to some of the services, resources, and tools that they provide on their platform. These have to be assessed in terms of their worth and whether the costs are necessary. Making some tolls premium may be an indicator of quality but not always. This is particularly the case when other platforms provide similar services toll-free.

Screening tools are particularly the ones that are bound to attract charges because they have abilities to analyze and assess market trends. They can do the thinking for the trader and help him in decision making. One has to read about the specifications of the tools and ascertain what they or cannot do. This is in order to know if they are customizable for the purpose of serving the needs and conveniences of traders.

Some charges can even be attached to the quotes update feed. Usually, the quotes can be accessed in real time for those who want to see them in real time. The quotes are important in influencing idea generation and sometimes can tip people of opportunities in the market. There is usually a delay for those who access the quotes updates for free.

It is also vital to understand platforms do not provide all the tools to everyone using their platform to trade. Some of the cutting-edge tools that can best serve the business interests of traders are premium. They have subscription charges or otherwise only appear on the accounts of traders who constantly sustain a certain threshold of account balance minimums. This is particularly the case for platforms that operate at the professional level. They require one to be active and remain active in trading since this serves the business interests of the brokerage through the commissions it earns on options contracts. In return, it offers the consultancy, expertise, and resource repository for one to realize value out of the options trades. This is why they attach a price on some of the tools.

Final Thoughts

One can only trust a platform that has a reputation for efficiency. This is a platform that ensures orders have a quick span of execution. This particularly for traders who understand the benefits of entering quick and instantly exiting from offered positions. The charges of platform subscription also matter. This is whether they are monthly or per year. It is vital to understand the way of earning waivers on platform fees. It could be through ensuring compliance with balance minimums or activity of trades per a set span of time.

Chapter : 4
Financial Leverage

Leverage is a concept that is used by both companies and investors. For investors, the notion of leverage is used to try and increase returns that come on investment. To use leverage, you have to make use of various instruments, including future, options, and margin accounts.

The use of leverage n options trading helps boost your profits. Trading in options can give you huge leverage and allow you to generate huge profits from a small investment.

Definition

Leverage is the ability to trade a large number of options using just a small amount of capital. Many traders feel that leverage is, but studies have found that the risk in leveraged options is nearly the same to non-leveraged securities.

Why Is Leverage Riskier?

Trading options using leverage is usually considered riskier because it exaggerates the potential of the business. For instance, you can use $500 to enter a trade that has a potential of $7000. Remember the first rule of trading – don't trade what you cannot lose.

This isn't as true as it seems, which is why it is vital that you know what you are doing at all times.

Leverage makes you utilize capital more efficiently. For this reason, many traders love the trade because it allows them to go for larger positions with limited capital.

When you use leverage, you don't reduce the potential profit that you will gain; rather, you reduce the risk in certain trades. For instance, if you want to put your money in 10,000 options at $8 per share, you would need to risk $80,000 worth of investment. This means that the whole amount of $80,000 would be at risk. However, you can use leverage to place a smaller amount of money, thus reducing the risk of loss.

This is the way you need to look at leverage, which is the right way.

Before you can trade leverage, you need to find a way to maximize the gains in each trade. Here are a few tips that you can explore:

Know When to Run

You need to cut losses early enough and then let your winning trades run to completion. Just the way you run other trades; you need to know when to cut your losses so that you don't end up bankrupt. You need to make use of stop losses when running leverage in trades.

Have a Stop Loss Set

As a trader, you need to determine your stop loss set so that you don't lose more than you can afford. The set that you come up with will depend upon the situation of the market at any time. Whatever the case, always make sure you have a set to guide you.

Don't Go With the Trade

Many traders try to chase a trade to the finish, something that ends up discouraging them and making them lose money. Once a move happens, you need to accept and wait for the next opening. Always be patient because just like the other opportunity came along, another one will definitely come by.

Have Limit Orders

Instead of placing market limits, opt for limit orders instead so that you can save on fees. The limit orders also help you reign in your emotions when you trade.

Learn About Technical Analysis

Make sure you learn about technical analysis before you jump into trading. Technical analysis will make sure you have the information that you need to make decisions fast.

The Advantages of Leverage in Options Trading

When you use leverage, you increase your financial capability as a trader and enjoy better trading results. You can change the amount of leverage at your discretion. This is because when you open a trading account, you have all the power of managing the amount of capital that you place on a trade. The good news is that you can use leverage free of charge, but you need to make sure you know how it works and whether it will work for you or not.

The level of leverage varies. Some trading platforms offer leverage from as low as 1:1 up to and beyond 1:1000. As a trader, it is advisable that you go for the largest leverage possible so that you can make the biggest returns.

Another advantage is that low leverage allows you as a new trader to survive. When starting out in options trading, you have the capacity to make small trades with little to show for your efforts. With leverage, you can make use of leverage to place trades that run into thousands of dollars without risking the same amount in terms of investment. As long as you know what you are doing, you have the capability to enjoy massive profits.

Disadvantages of Leverage in Options Trading

As much as it is a good way to make huge profits, you also need to understand that leverage comes with many demerits. These include:

Magnifies the Losses

With leverage, you will be faced with huge losses if the trade decides to go the other way. And since the original outlay is way smaller than what you end up losing, many traders forget that they are placing their capital at risk. Make sure you come up with a ratio that will help protect your interests and then know how to manage trade risk.

No Privileges

When you use leverage to trade, you sacrifice full ownership of the asset. For instance, when you use leverage, you give up the opportunity of enjoying dividends. This is because the amount on the dividend is deducted from the account regardless of the position of the trade.

Margin Calls

A margin call is when the lender asks you to add funds so that you keep the trade open. You have to decide whether you wish to add funds or exit a position to reduce the exposure.

Incur Expenses

When you use leverage to trade options, you will receive the money from the lender so that you can use the full position.

Most traders opt to keep their positions open overnight, which attracts a fee to cover the costs.

How Much Leverage Do You Need in Options Trading

Knowing how to trade options needs detailed knowledge about the various aspects of economics. For many people, the lack of knowledge to use leverage is the major cause of losses.

Studies show that many traders who opt for options lose money in the process. This happens whether for smaller or high leverage.

Risks of High Leverage

In options trading, the capital for placing a trade is usually sourced from a broker. While you have the ability to borrow huge amounts to place on a trade, you can gain more if the trade is successful.

A few years back, traders were able to offer leverages of up to 400 times the initial capital. However, rules and regulations have been, and at the moment, you can only access 50 times what you have. For instance, if you have $1000, you can control up to $50,000.

Choosing the Right Leverage

You need to look at different factors when choosing the kind of leverage that will work for you.

First, you need to start with low levels of leverage, because the more you borrow, the more you will need to pay back. Second, you need to use stops to make sure you protect the amount you have borrowed. Remember losses won't go down well with you.

All in all, you need to choose leverage which you find is comfortable for you. If you are a beginner, go for low leverage so that you minimize risks. If you know what you are doing, then go for maximum leverage to build your returns.

Using stops on order allows you to reduce loses when the trade changes direction. As a newbie, this is the only protection you need to make it in the market. This is because you will learn about the trades and how to place them while limiting any losses that might arise.

How to Manage Risk in Options Trading

Options trading comes with a number of risks that you need to manage so that you can enjoy the profits and minimize losses.

Here are a few risks and how to deal with them.

Losing More than What You Have

This risk is inherent in options trading, especially if you are using leverage to make a trade. It means that you put up a small fraction of the initial deposit to open the trade. This means that your fate is in the hands of the direction of the market. If it goes along with your prediction, you will gain more than the deposit. On the other hand, if the direction changes and you lose the position, you might end up losing more than your initial deposit.

When this happens, you need to have a strategy in place to help mitigate the risk. What you need to do in this case is to set a limit, so that you define the exact level at which the trade should stop so that you don't lose more than you can handle.

Positions Closing Unexpectedly

When positions close unexpectedly, they lead to loss of money. To keep the trades open, you need to have some money in the account. This aspect is called the margin, and if you don't have enough funds to cover the margin, then the position might close.

To mitigate this, you need to keep an eye on the running balances and always add funds as needed.

Sudden Huge Losses or Gains

The market can turn out to be volatile, and when it does, you need to move fast. Markets change depending on the news or something else in the market, which can be an announcement, event, or changes in trader behavior.

Apart from having stops, you also need to get notifications regarding any upcoming movement, which tells you whether to react or not,

Orders Filled in Erroneously

When you give instructions to a broker to place a trade for you, and the broker instead does the opposite. This is termed slippage. When this happens, use guaranteed stops to make sure you protect yourself against any slippage that might occur.

How to Trade Smarter Using Leverage

Even with leverage in tow, you need to have a way to trade better. With many mistakes occurring during a trade, you stand to lose more than gain if you don't have the right tips to excel. Let us look at the top mistakes that you go through to get to the top.

Misunderstanding Leverage

Many beginners don't understand leverage and go ahead to misuse this feature, barely realizing the risk they are exposing themselves to.

To make this work for you, learn about leverage, and master it. Understand what it is and what it isn't and then find out the best ways to make use of it. You also need to understand how much you can put in without running huge losses.

Having No Exit Plan

Just like socks, you need to control your emotions when trading options. It doesn't mean that you have to swallow your greed and fear; rather, you need to have a plan that you can go with. Once you have a plan, you need to stick to it so that even when things aren't going your way, you have something to guide you to make a recovery.

You need to have an exit plan, which means you know when to drop a trade.

Failure to Try New Strategies

You need to make sure you try out a few new strategies depending on the level of trading you want to achieve. Most traders get a single strategy and then stick to it even when it is not working out for them. When this happens, you are often tempted to go against the rules that you set down.

Maintain an open mind so that you can learn new option trading strategies to help you get more out of your trades.

Chapter : 5
The Basics of Technical Analysis

Technical analysis is the method of using charts and other recording methods to analyze various data in options trading. Using these visual instruments, you have the chance to determine the direction of the market because they give you a trend.

This method focuses on studying the supply and demand of a market. The price will be seen to rise when the investor realizes the market is undervalued, and this leads to buying. If they think that the market is overvalued, the prices will start falling, and this is deemed the perfect time to sell.

You need to understand the movement of the various indicators to make the perfect decision. This method works on the premise that history usually repeats itself – a huge change in the prices affects the investors in any situation.

History

Technical analysis has been used over the years in trades. The technical analysis methods have been used for over a hundred years to come up with deductions regarding the market.

In Asia, the use of technical analysis led to the development of candlestick techniques, and it forms the main charting techniques.

Over time, more tools and techniques have come up to help traders come up with predictions of the prices in various markets.

There are many indicators that you can use to determine the direction of the market, but only a few are valuable to your course. Let us look at the various indicators and how to use them.

Support and Resistance

These levels occur at points where both the buyer and the seller aren't dormant. These levels are displayed on the chart using a horizontal line extended in the past to the future.

The different prices reach at the support and resistance points in the future.

How to Apply Support and Resistance

- Using these points allows you to know when to call or put.
- Support and resistance give you a way to determine the entry point to use for a directional trade.

The Significance of Trends in Option Trading

Technical analysis works on the premise of the trend. These trends come by due to the interaction of the buyer and the seller. The aggressiveness of one of the parties in the market will determine how steep the trend becomes. To make a profit, you have to take advantage of the changes in the price movement.

To understand the direction of the trend, you ought to look at the troughs and peaks and how they relate to each other.

When looking for money in options trading, you ought to trade with a trend. The trend is what determines the decision you make when faced with a situation – whether to buy or to sell. You need to know the various signs that a prevailing trend is soon ending so that you can manage the risks and exit the trades the right way.

Characteristics of Technical Analysis

This analysis makes use of models and trading rules using different price and volume changes. These include the volume, price, and other different market info.

Technical analysis is applied among financial professionals and traders and is used by many option traders.

The Principles of Technical analysis

Many traders on the market use the price to come up with information that affects the decision you make ultimately. The analysis looks at the trading pattern and what information it offers you rather than looking at drivers such as news events, economic and fundamental events.

Price action usually tends to change every time because the investor leans towards a certain pattern, which in turn predicts trends and conditions.

Prices Determine Trends

Technical analysts know that the price in the market determines the trend of the market. The trend can be up, down, or move sideways.

History Usually Repeats Itself

Analysts believe that an investor repeats the behavior of the people that traded before them. The investor sentiment usually repeats itself. Due to the fact that the behavior repeats itself, traders know that using a price pattern can lead to predictions.

The investor uses the research to determine if the trend will continue or if the reversal will stop eventually and will anticipate a change when the charts show a lot of investor sentiment.

Combination with Other Analysis Methods

To make the most out of the technical analysis, you need to combine it with other charting methods on the market. You also need to use secondary data, such as sentiment analysis and indicators.

To achieve this, you need to go beyond pure technical analysis, and combine other market forecast methods in line with technical work. You can use technical analysis along with fundamental analysis to improve the performance of your portfolio.

You can also combine technical analysis with economics and quantitative analysis. For instance, you can use neural networks along with technical analysis to identify the relationships in the market. Other traders make use of technical analysis with astrology.

Other traders go for newspaper polls, sentiment indicators to come with deductions.

The Different Types of Charts Used in Technical Analysis

Candlestick Chart

This is a charting method that came from the Japanese. The method fills the interval between opening and closing prices to show a relationship. These candles use color coding to show the closing points. You will come across black, red, white, blue, or green candles to represent the closing point at any time.

Open-high-low-close Chart (OHLC)

These are also referred to as bar charts, and they give you a connection between the maximum and minimum prices in a trading period. They usually feature a tick on the left side to show the open price and one on the right to show the closing price.

Line Chart

This is a chart that maps the closing price values using a line segment.

Point and Figure Chart

This employs numerical filters that reference times without fully using the time to construct the chart.

Overlays

These are usually used on the main price charts and come in different ways:

- *Resistance* – refers to a price level that acts as the maximum level above the usual price
- *Support* – the opposite of resistance, and it shows as the lowest value of the price
- *Trend line* – this is a line that connects two troughs or peaks.
- *Channel* – refers to two trend lines that are parallel to each other

- *Moving average* – a kind of dynamic trendline that looks at the average price in the market
- *Bollinger bands* – these are charts that show the rate of volatility in a market.
- *Pivot point* – this refers to the average of the high, low, and closing price averages for a certain stock or currency.

Price-based Indicators

These analyze the price values of the market. These include:

- *Advance decline line* – this is an indicator of the market breadth
- *Average directional index* – shows the strength of a trend in the market
- *Commodity channel index* – helps you to identify cyclical trends in the market
- *Relative strength index* – this is a chart that shows you the strength of the price
- *Moving average convergence (MACD)* – this shows the point where two trend line converge or diverge.
- *Stochastic oscillator* – this shows the close position that has happened within the recent trading range
- *Momentum* – this is a chart that tells you how fast the price changes

The Benefits of Technical Analysis in Options Trading

There are a variety of benefits that you enjoy when you use technical analysis in trading options. The benefits arise from the fact that traders are usually asking a lot of questions touching on the price of the market and entry points. While the forecast for prices is a huge task, the use of technical analysis makes it easier to handle.

The major advantages of technical analysis include

Expert Trend Analysis

This is the biggest advantage of technical analysis in any market. With this method, you can predict the direction of the market at any time. You can determine whether the market will move up, down or sideways easily.

Entry and Exit Points

As a trader, you need to know when to place a trade and when to opt out. The entry point is all about knowing the right time to enter the trade for good returns. Exiting a trade is also vital because it allows you to reduce losses.

Leverage Early Signals

Every trader looks for ways to get early signals to assist them in making decisions. Technical analysis gives you signals to trigger a decision on your part. This is usually ideal when you suspect that a trend will reverse soon. Remember the time the trend reverses are when you need to make crucial decisions.

It Is Quick

In options trading, you need to go with techniques that give you fast results. Additionally, getting technical analysis data is cheaper than other techniques in fundamental analysis, with some companies offering free charting programs. If you are in the market to make use of short time intervals such as 1-minute, 5-minute, 30 minute or 1-hour charts, you can get this using technical analysis.

It Gives You A Lot of Information

Technical analysis gives you a lot of information that you can use to make trading decisions. You can easily build a position depending on the information you get then take or exit trades. You have access to information such as chart pattern, trends, support, resistance, market momentum, and other information.

The current price of an asset usually reflects every known information of an asset. While the market might be rife with rumors that the prices might surge or plummet, the current price represents the final point for all information. As the traders and investors change their bearing from one part to another, the changes in asset reflect the current value perception.

If all this turns out to be true, then the only info you require is a price chart that gives all the price reflections and predictions. There isn't any need for you to worry yourself with the reasons why the price is rising or falling when you can use a chart to determine everything.

With the right technical analysis information, you can make trading easier and faster because you make decisions based not on hearsay but facts. You don't have to spend your time reading and trying to make headway in financial news. All you need us to check what the chart tells you.

You Understand Trends

If the prices on the market were to gyrate randomly without any direction, you would find it hard to make money. While these trends run in all directions, the prices always move in trends. Directional bias allows you to leverage the benefits of making money. Technical analysis allows you to determine when a trend occurs and when it doesn't occur, or when it is in reversal.

Many of the profitable techniques that are used by the traders to make money follow trends. This means that you find the right trend and then look for opportunities that allow you to enter the market in the same direction as the trend. This helps you to capitalize on the price movement.

Trends run in various degrees. The degree of the trend determines how much money you make, whether in the short term or long-term trading. Technical analysis gives you all the tools that make it possible for you to do this.

History Always Repeats Itself

Technical analysis uses common patterns to give you the information to trade. However, you need to understand that history will not be exact when it repeats itself, though. The current analysis will be either bigger or smaller, depending on the existing market conditions. The only thing is that it won't be a replica of the prior pattern.

This pans out easily because most human psychology doesn't change so much, and you will see that the emotions have a hand in making sure that prices rise and fall. The emotions that traders exhibit create a lot of patterns that lead to changes in prices all the time. As a trader, you need to identify these patterns and then use them for trading. Use prior history to guide you and then the current price as a trigger of the trade.

Enjoy Proper Timing

Do you know that without proper timing you will not be able to make money at all? One of the major advantages of technical analysis is that you get the chance to time the trades. Using technical analysis, you get to wait, then place your money in other opportunities until it is the right time to place a trade.

Applicable Over a Wide Time Frame

When you learn technical analysis, you get to apply it to many areas in different markets, including options. All the trading in a market is based mostly on the patters that are as a result of human behavior. These patterns can then be mapped out on a chart to be used across the markets.

While there is some difference between analyzing different securities, you will be able to use technical analysis in most of the markets.

Additionally, you can use the analysis in any timeframe, which is applicable whether you use hourly, daily, or weekly charts. These markets are usually taken to be fractal, which essentially means that patterns that appear on a small scale will also be present on a large scale as well.

Technical Analysis Secrets to Become the Best Trader

To make use of technical analysis the right way, you need to follow time-testing approaches that have made the technique a gold mine for many traders. Let us look at the various tips that will take you from novice to pro in just a few days:

Use More than One Indicator

Numbers make trading easy, but it also applies to the way you apply your techniques. For one, you need to know that just because one technical indicator is better than using one, applying a second indicator is better than using just one. The use of more than one indicator is one of the best ways to confirm a trend. It also increases the odds of being right.

As a trader, you will never be 100 percent right at all times, and you might even find that the odds are stashed against you when everything is plain to see. However, don't demand too much from your indicators such that you end up with analysis paralysis.

To achieve this, make use of indicators that complement each other rather than the ones that clash against each other.

Go For Multiple Time Frames

Using the same buy signal every day allows you to have confidence that the indicator is giving you all you need to know to trade. However, make sure you look for a way to use multiple timeframes to confirm a trend. When you have a doubt, it is wise that you increase the timeframe from an hour to a day or from a daily chart to a weekly chart.

Understand that No Indicator Measures Everything

You need to know that indicators are supposed to show how strong a trend is, they won't tell you much more. So, you need to understand and focus on what the indicator is supposed to communicate instead of working with assumptions.

Go With the Trend

If you notice that an option is trading upward, then go ahead and buy it. Conversely when the trend stops trending, then it is time to sell it. If you aren't sure of what is going on in the market at that time, then don't make a move.

However, waiting might make you lose profitable trades as opposed to trading. You also miss out on opportunities to create more capital.

Have the Right Skills

It really takes superior analytical capabilities and real skill to be successful at trading, just like any other endeavor. Many people think that it is hard to make money with options trading, but with the right approach, you can make extraordinary profits.

You need to learn and understand the various skills so that you know what the market seeks from you and how to achieve your goals.

Trade with a Purpose

Many traders go into options trading with the main aim of having a hobby. Well, this way you won't be able to make any money at all. What you need to do is to trade for the money – strive to make profits unlike those who try to make money as a hobby.

Always Opt for High value

Well, no one tells you to trade any security that comes your way – it is purely a matter of choice. Try and go for high-value options so that you can trade them the right way. Make use of fundamental analysis to choose the best options to trade in.

Be Disciplined

When using technical analysis, you might find yourself in situations that require you to make a decision fast. To achieve success, you need to have strict risk management protocols. Don't base on your track record to come up with choices; instead, make sure you follow what the analysis tells you.

Don't Overlook Your Trading Plan

The trading plan is in place to guide you when things go awry. Coming up with the plan is easy, but many people find it hard to implement the plan the right way. The trading plan has various components – the signals and the take-profit/stop-loss rules. Once you get into the market, you need to control yourself because you have already taken a leap. Remember you cannot control the indicators once they start running – all you can do is to prevent yourself from messing up everything.

Come up with the trading rules when you are unemotional to try and mitigate the effects of making bad decisions.

Accept Losses

Many people trade with one thing in mind – losses aren't part of their plan. This is a huge mistake because you need to understand that every trade has two sides to it – a loss and a profit. Remember that the biggest mistake that leads to losses isn't anything to do with bad indicators rather using them the wrong way. Always have a stop-loss order when you trade to prevent loss of money.

Have a Target When You Trade

So, what do you plan to achieve today? Remember, trading is a way to grow your capital as opposed to saving. Options trading is a business that has probable outcomes that you get to estimate. When you make a profit, make sure you take some money from the table and then put it in a safe place.

How to Apply Technical Analysis

Many traders have heard of technical analysis, but they don't know how to use it to make deductions and come up with decisions that impact their trades. Here are the different steps to make sure you have the right decision when you use technical analysis.

1. *Identify a Trend*

You need to identify an option and then see whether there is a trend or not. The trend might be driving the options up or down. The market is bullish if it is moving up and bearish when it is moving down. As a trader, you need to go along with the trend instead of fighting it. When you fight against the trend, you incur unnecessary losses that will make it hard to achieve the rewards that you seek.

You also need to have good ways to identify the trend; this is because the market has the capacity to move in a certain direction. It is not all about identifying the direction of the trend but also when the trend is moving out of the trend.

So, how can you identify a trend the right way? Here are some tools to use so as to get the right trend:

- Using triangles that map major swings
- The Bill Williams Fractals indicator helps you to identify the trend
- Use the moving average
- Trend lines give you an idea of the direction of the trend

Once you identify the trend, the next step is to try and mark the support and resistance levels

2. *Support and Resistance Levels*

You need to understand the support and resistance levels that are within the trend. Use the Fibonacci retracement tool to identify these spots on the trend.

3. *Look for Patterns*

Patterns need to show you what to expect in a certain market. You can use candlesticks to determine the chart pattern.

Chapter : 6
Mindset: Controlling Your Emotions (Trading Psychology)

GBP/USD	82%	1.54260	14:15		04:21
EUR/JPY	82%	135.365	14:15		04:21
GBP/JPY	81%	183.543	14:15		04:21
USD/JPY	73%	118.983	14:15		04:21
USD/CAD	79%	1.25174	14:15		04:21
USD/CHF	73%	0.94890	14:15		04:21
EUR/GBP	78%	0.73751	14:15		04:21
AUD/USD	79%	0.77801	14:15		04:21
AUD/NZD	73%	1.03561	14:15		04:21
NZD/USD	73%	0.75125	14:15		04:21

Trading psychology is the mental state and emotions that determine the success or failure of trading options. It represents the aspect of your behavior that dictates the decisions you make when faced with a trade. The psychology is vital to any trade and can be compared to experience, knowledge, and skills in determining your success as a trader.

When you decide to start options trading, you need to grasp the concept of risk-taking and discipline that determine the implementation of any trade.

The two most common emotions are greed and fear, while others are regret and hope.

The Basics of Trading Psychology

We associate trading psychology to some behaviors and emotions that are often the triggers for catalysts for decisions. The most common emotions that every trader will come across is fear and greed.

Fear

At any given time, fear represents one of the worst kinds of emotions that you can have. Check in your newspaper one day, and you read about a steep selloff, and the next thing is trying to rack your brain about what to do next even if it isn't the right action at that time.

Many investors think that they know what will happen in the next few days, which makes them have a lot of confidence in the outcome of the trade. This leads to investors getting into the trade at a level that is too high or too low, which in turn makes them react emotionally.

As the trader puts a lot of hope on the single trade, the level of fear tends to increase, and hesitation and caution kick in.

Fear is part of every trader, but skilled traders have the capacity to manage the fear. There are various types of fears that you will experience, let us look at a few of them:

The Fear to Lose

Have you ever entered a trade and all you could think about is losing? The fear of losing makes it hard for you to execute the perfect strategy or enter or exit a strategy at the right time.

As a trader, you know that you need to make timely decisions when the strategy signals you to take one. When you have fear guiding you, the level of confidence drops, and you don't have the ability to execute the strategy the right way, at the right time. When a strategy fails, you lose trust in your abilities as well as strategy.

When you lose trust in many of the strategies, you end up with analysis paralysis, whereby you don't have the capacity to pull the trigger on any decision that you make. Making a move becomes a huge challenge.

When you cannot pull the trigger, all you can think about is staying away from the pain of losing, while you need to move towards gains.

No trader likes to lose, but it is a fact that even the best traders will make losses once in a while. The key is for them to make more profitable trades that allow them to stay in the game.

When you worry too much, you end up being distracted from your execution process, and instead, you focus on the results.

To reduce the fear in trading, you need to accept losses. The probability of losing or making a profit is 50/50, and you need to accept this fact and accept a trade, whether it is a sell or a buy signal.

The Fear of a Positive Trend Going Negative (and Vice Versa)

Many traders choose to go for quick profits and then leave the losses to run down. Many traders want to convince themselves that they have made some money for the day, so they tend to go for a quick profit so that they have the winning feeling.

So, what should you do instead? You need to stick with the trend. When you notice a trend is starting, it is good to stay with the trend until you have a signal that the trend is about to reverse. It is only then that you exit this position.

To understand this concept, you need to consider the history of the market. History is good at pointing out that times change, and trends can go either way. Remember that no one knows the exact time the trend will start or end; all you need to do is wait upon the signal.

The Fear of Missing Out

For every trade, you have people that doubt the capacity of the trade to go through. After you place the trade, you will be faced with many skeptics that will doubt the whole procedure and leave you wondering whether to exit the strategy or not.

This fear is also characterized by greed – because you aren't working on the premise of making a successful trade rather the fact that the security is rising without you having a piece of the pie.

This fear is usually based on information that there is a trend which you missed that you would have capitalized on.

This fear has a downside – you will forget about any potential risk associated with the trade and instead think that you have the capacity to make a profit because other people benefited from the action.

Fear of Being Wrong

Many traders put too much emphasis on being right that they forget that this is a business they should run the right way. They also forget that being successful is all about knowing the trend and how it affects their engagement.

When you follow the best timing strategy, you create many positive results over a certain time.

The uncanny desire to focus on always being right instead of focusing on making money is a great part of your ego, and to stay on the right path; you need to trade without your ego for once.

If you accommodate a perfectionist mentality when you get into trades, you will be after failure because you will experience a lot of losses as well. Perfectionists don't take losses the right way, and this translates into fear.

Ways to Overcome Fear in Trading

As you can see, it is obvious that fear can lead to losses. So, how can you avoid this fear and become successful?

- *Learn*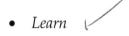

You need to find a way to get knowledge so that you have the basis for making decisions. When you know all there is to know about options, you know what to buy and when to sell, and learn which ones to watch. You are then more comfortable making the right decisions.

- *Have Goals*

What are your short term and long-term goals? Setting the right goals helps you to overcome fear. When you have goals, you have rules that dictate how you behave, even in times of fear. You also have a timeline for your journey.

- *Envision the Bigger Picture*

You always need to evaluate your choices at all times and see what you have gained or lost so far for taking some steps. Understanding the mistakes, you made gives you guidance to make better decisions in the future.

- *Start Small*

Many traders that subscribe to fear have lost a lot before. They put a lot of funds on the line and ended up losing, which in turn made them fear to place other trades. Begin with small sums so that you don't risk too much to put fear in you. Once you get more confident, you can invest larger sums so that you enjoy more profit.

- *Use the Right Strategy*

Having the right trading strategy makes it easy to execute your trades successfully. Make sure you look at various options trading strategies so that you know which one is ideal for your situation and skills.

Many strategies can help you succeed, but others might leave you confused. If you have a strategy that doesn't give you the returns you desire, then adjust it to suit your needs over time. Refine it till you are comfortable with its performance.

- *Go Simple*

When you have a strategy that is simple and straightforward, you will be less likely to lose confidence along the way because you know what to expect.

Additionally, the easier the strategy, the faster it will be to spot any issues.

- *Don't Hesitate*

At times you have to jump into the fray even if you aren't so comfortable with the way it works. Once you begin taking steps, you will learn more about the trade.

However, you need always to be prepared when taking any trade. The more prepared you are, the easier it will be for you to run successful trades.

- *Don't Give Up*

Things might not always go as you expect them to do. Remember that mistakes are there to give you lessons that will make you a better trader. When you lose, take time to identify the mistake you made and then correct it, then try again.

Greed

This refers to a selfish desire to get more money than you need from a trade. When the desire to get more than you can usually make takes over your decision-making process, you are looking at failure.

Greed is seen to be more detrimental than fear. Yes, fear can make you lose trades, but the good thing is that you get to preserve your capital. On the other hand, greed places you in a situation where you spend your capital faster than you return it. It pushes you to act when you shouldn't be acting at all.

The Danger of Being Greedy

When you are greedy, you end up acting irrationally. Irrational trading behavior can be overtrading, overleveraging, holding onto trades for too long, or chasing different markets.

The more greed you have, the more foolish you act. If you reach a point at which greed takes over from common sense, then you are overdoing it.

When you are greedy, you also end up risking way much more than you can handle and you end up with a loss. You also have unrealistic expectations from the market, which makes it seem as if you are after just money and nothing else.

When you are greedy, you also start trading prematurely without any knowledge of the options trading market.

When you are too greedy, your judgment is clouded, and you won't think about any negative consequences that might result when you make certain decisions.

Many traders that were too greedy ended up giving up after making this mistake in the initial trading phase.

How to Overcome Greed

Like any other endeavors in trading, you need a lot of efforts to overcome greed. It might not be easy because we are talking about human emotions here, but it is possible.

First, you have to know that every call you make won't be the right one at all times. There are times when you won't make the right move, and you will end up losing money. At times you will miss the perfect strategy altogether, and you won't move a step ahead.

Secondly, you have to agree that the market is way bigger than you. When you do this, you will accept and make mistakes in the process.

Hope

Hope is what keeps a trading expectation alive when it has reached reversal. Hope is usually factored in the mind of a trader that has placed a huge amount on a trade. Many traders also go for hope when they wish to recoup past losses. These traders are always hopeful that the next trade will be the best, and they end up placing more than they should on the trade.

This type of emotion is dangerous because the market doesn't care at all about your hopes and will take your money.

Regret

This is the feeling of disappointment or sadness over a trade that has been done, especially when it has resulted in a loss.

Focusing too much on missing on trade makes the trader not to move forward. After you learn the lessons after such a loss, you need to understand the mistakes you made then move ahead.

When you decide to let regret to rule your thinking, you start chasing markets with the hopes that you will end up making money on a position by doubling the entrance price.

Things That Distinguish Winning and Losing Traders in Options Trading

Handling Analysis Paralysis

Traders usually start their journey getting the right knowledge. This knowledge comes in the form of books, coaches, and more. Once you have the information, the next step is to take it and use it in the market. The lucky ones will place various trades, and then things will go their way, while for others, the money will go down the drain.

Trading requires you to determine the right time to place a trade or exit one. The successful trader will know when to use a strategy, but the losing trader will end up placing trade after trade without any success at all.

Understanding the Nature of the Market

You need to understand that no market is constant – it changes with time. At times, the market will go along with your analysis, while at times; it might go the opposite direction.

Accept the Risk

No one wants to lose money on the markets. You need to come up with a strategy that allows you to know when to stop and reflect or tap out. At times you have to pull the plug regardless of how much you have invested in research and your expectations.

Know When to Take Profits

So, what determines the exit strategy? You need to know what point requires you to say this profit is enough for me. At times, it might be dictated by the changes in the trend or your rules of trading. Don't hold on to a trade for too long because it is always better to have some profit than wait and end up losing everything.

Understanding When you are Wrong

You need to remember that the options trading market is random, and you need to admit when you are wrong at times. This is because failure to admit will lead you to greed that might cloud your judgment.

When it comes to trading options, you have various traps that lead to fear or greed. Most of these traps come on expiration day; let us look at the various traps to avoid.

Traps to Avoid On Expiration Day

So, it is the day when the options are expiring, and this is the time you have to decide what action to take. If you are a seller, then you are anticipating this time because you hope to make some money out of the trade, while if you are a buyer, then you are dreading due to losses that might arise.

Either way, you need to be privy to some aspects of trading that will help you avoid any surprises.

Here are top traps that you need to know and avoid at this time.

1   Exercising the Long Option

You need to consider your options at expiration. At times, you can just close the options trade rather than buying the shares. Remember that when you exercise your options, you have to pay additional broker commissions that might not be ideal for you.

2   Options Vary From Country to Country

A huge percentage of the traders on the market use American style options to trade. However, other traders desire to trade the European options and this com with differences.

For European options, you can only exercise the option at the time of expiration, while American options give you the chance to exercise the option between the time you show interest till expiration.

For both options, you don't have to be stuck with the position till the expiry.

3   Holding Positions to the Last Minute

One of the hardest things to do is letting go of a position that you believe in. There are two scenarios under this – first, you have a losing trade that you just don't want to let go. On the other hand, you might have a position that is making you some money, but you think you have the chance to get more money before the options expire.

When it comes to trading, the final few days are the worst times to exit the trade because of the high risk that is associated with it. This means that the value of the option swings in any direction during these final days. Due to this, you can see your profits disappear in a few seconds!

The good thing is that you can decide to let the options go worthless and retain the premium that you collect at expiration.

4   Rolling an Option Position

Most investors are convinced that certain security if way better than another one. Many stock traders think that stock trading is much better than the options because they tend to expire.

If you are on a winning streak, don't hold out longer just to see the close; instead take the chance of closing the deal and making some money, however little. Using the rolling technique, you get to lock the profits in a position and then benefit from the profit. You can do this way early in the trading cycle as opposed to going after it when you need to close the trade.

Rolling gives you the ability to make some profits then use the original investment to pay for another option with a longer expiration period.

Chapter : 7
Options Trading Strategies for Beginners

Whether you are a beginner, average trader, or experienced options trader, there are strategies you need to use to make options work for you. When it comes to options trading, you do not need to be a genius to make it.

Many traders invest in options without the necessary information. This is one mistake that results in self-doubt and lack of confidence in the trade. People who do this often give up as soon as they start. With the right strategies in place, you can easily make income, secure your capital, and make the volatile nature of options to work in your favor.

95

Trading strategies help you reduce risks and maximize profits. If you do not have any strategy to follow, the business can become difficult and costly. Options strategies vary from simple ones to sophisticated ones but have one thing in common – they are all based on put and call operations. The payoffs do vary greatly, and before you settle on a strategy, be sure to understand how it works, the expected gain as well as if there are any risks involved. As a beginner, do not get overwhelmed with a large number of strategies available since you only need a few basic ones to get started. You can add more of these to your trading plan as you master the game.

This book focuses on some of the most popular basic strategies in the industry. Generally, options trading strategies can be divided into three categories - conservative long-term strategies, semi-conservative or short-term, also known as aggressive strategies.

- Conservative strategies are accomplished on a long-term basis. These allow you to build your capital in a slow but steady process. The benefit of such strategies is that they reduce the risk of losing your capital.
- Semi-conservative strategies consist of four to six trades per day. These are more aggressive than conservative strategies and involve more risk as well.

- Aggressive strategies allow numerous trades each day. These often result in higher risks and small profits.

With this in mind, you are able to define the type of strategies you need. If you are a day trader, then aggressive strategies will suit you better. Now, let us look at some of the strategies you need to understand to get started in options trading.

Strategies Related to Calls

The process of buying and selling of calls is one of the easiest in the options trading field. It is actually one of the popular and frequently used ways to get into options trading. This is because it allows you to own stock, using very little capital. Buying calls also presents you with a higher profit potential than purchasing stock. Some of the strategies you can exploit when buying calls are listed below.

Covered Calls

Covered calls entail setting up call options against your own stock. This strategy is not only popular in options trading but in other financial institutes that deal with stock as well. In this strategy, you only sell options to protect your stock from downward price movement and also increase your returns. Most investors do this any time there is a possibility of good gains on their stock. In most cases, they sell out-of-the-money calls, and once the price goes high, they trade the stock for a profit.

One advantage of this strategy is that you get to keep your stock at expiration if it falls below the strike price. If the stock goes above the strike price, you will sell the stock shares to the buyer at the strike price. Most investors use this strategy to generate profit at limited risks while retaining their stock.

The downside of covered calls is that you need at least 100 shares of stock to make the calls. The strategy is thus not beneficial for traders who wish to start small. Traders are also allowed to sell only one call option against 100 stock shares. This is called a covered call because, in the event that the stock price goes high, the call will be covered by the position of your stock.

You can consider using this strategy to make a profit if you already have the required stock and do not expect its cost to go high in the near future.

Bull Call Spread

In this strategy, you purchase calls continuously and at specific strike prices then sell these calls at higher strike prices. Normally, the calls have the same expiration time and are related to the same underlying security. Investors use this strategy when there is an expected rise in the cost of the underlying asset, especially during high volatile periods. When used correctly, it reduces the trader's upside and lowers the premium spent as compared to buying covered calls.

The strategy lowers the cost of a call option and defines a limit within which the investor can generate income. Here is the procedure of applying the bull call spread strategy:

- Select an asset that has the potential to appreciate in days, weeks or months
- Purchase a call option at a strike price that is higher than the current market price. Specify the expiration date and make a payment for the premium.
- Sell a call option at a price that is higher than the strike price, but with the same expiration date as the initial call option. Do this simultaneously until the expiration time is reached.

By simultaneously selling call options, you will be able to receive a profit that will offset what you paid for the long or first call.

Since the strategy operates within limits, profits and losses are often constrained to certain amounts. This eliminates the possibility of losing all your stock to the trade. However, the disadvantage of this is that you cannot obtain any gain that is beyond the strike price of the sold call options.

Long Call

This strategy allows you to buy a call while expecting the prices to go beyond the strike price during expiration. One great advantage of this strategy is that if the prices go higher than the striking price, you can earn multiple times the initial premium since the trade has no upper limit. As the stock rises, the call keeps going higher. It is for this particular reason that long calls are common amongst traders who wish to make a profit from rising stock prices.

A disadvantage of this strategy is that if the expiration is reached and your stock is below the strike price, you may lose your entire premium. Therefore, use this strategy only when you are sure that the costs will keep rising until the option expires. If the stock rises only by a small percentage, you may lose part of the premium.

Long Call Butterfly Spread

This strategy combines the bull spread strategy and the bear spread strategy. These two strategies converge at the same strike price. Therefore, the long call butterfly strategy makes use of three strike prices. Just like the bull call spread, this strategy requires that you use call options derived from the same asset, and having the same expiration date.

Because the strategy allows you to sell two options at the same strike price, it is considered one of the low-price strategies that beginners can take advantage of. However, since it utilizes spreads of long and short calls, the chances of getting large profits are relatively slim. If the strike price is higher than the premium, the trade is considered to be bullish, and if it is lower than the premium, it is a bearish trade.

Short Call

In the short call strategy, you are required to sell your stock at a certain striking price assigned to the option. The main target of this strategy is for the call to expire worthlessly. The stock price must remain below the strike price for you to realize a profit. You risk losing your premium if the stock rises. Most traders only use this strategy when there is a high probability that the stock price will diminish. The more it rises, the more you lose money.

Related to this is the short call butterfly spread that involves selling one call option at low striking prices, buying two at-the-money call options, and then selling one out-of-the-money call option with a higher strike price. Profit is realized when the underlying stock's price rises over the higher striking price or goes below, the lower strike price during expiration.

Strategies Related to Puts

Buying of puts is one strategy you should use anytime you notice the market taking a direction that is against your call options. Traders buy puts whenever there is a possibility of the prices going down. Buying puts the opposite of buying calls. Here are some strategies related to the put option that may be of benefit.

Cash Secured Puts

This is the opposite of covered calls. This strategy requires you to sell puts against a liquid cash balance in your broker account. The only people who use this strategy are investors anticipating a decline in the stock price or those traders who wish to generate some profit from excess cash that is in their possession. Through selling puts against their cash, they are able to make some profit.

Generally, this strategy involves selling put options while saving enough cash on the side to purchase the underlying stock. It allows you to get stock options at discounted prices and sell them at a profit. The goal is to acquire the underlying stock at a price that is below the market price.

When the stock goes below the strike price, the put is assigned, and the trader allowed to buy the stock at the strike price. The process involves a lot of risks since the stock may decrease way below the strike price and this means that you may be required to purchase the shares at an amount that is above the current stock price. This comes as a loss to you, especially if the prices keep going down.

Married Put

This is where an investor buys stock and equivalent put options simultaneously. You can sell the put option at the strike price. Just like the covered call, each married put contract requires 100 shares. In this case, the trader is positive that the stock value will rise but uses a put option as insurance should the value go down.

The married put strategy is common in investors who have a vision of minimizing the downside risk of their stock. When an investor buys the shares and an option, he protects his stock from loss should a negative event occur and also makes some cash as the stock's value increases. However, if the stock does not go down, the investor loses the cash placed on the put option as a premium.

The married put has so many similarities with the covered call. It gets its name from combining or marrying a put option with the underlying stock. For every 100 shares, you are only allowed to buy one put option.

The maximum profit for this strategy is undefined. The more the stock appreciates, the higher the profits. One downside of this strategy lies in the cost of premiums. The put option increases in value as the stock value declines, and because of this, the trader loses the cost placed on the option. Such losses, however, cannot be compared to the value of the underlying stock which would have been saved in the process.

Long Put

Here, the trader purchases a put while expecting the prices to go below the strike price at expiration. It gives you the opportunity to multiply your initial investments in case the stock value falls at zero.

The long put has various similarities to the long call. The only difference is that you are expecting the prices to decline rather than go up. The upside of the long put is similar to that of the long call because the put option's value is capable of increasing in bounds. However, in this case, the stock should not go on the upside.

This strategy helps minimize the risk involved in shorting of stock. You must, however, note that if expiration is reached when the stock is above the strike price, the put option will be worthless and you will gain no profit.

The long-put strategy is ideal for use when you expect the stock price to fall before the expiration of the put option. The fall must be significant for you to return the premium paid; otherwise, you will end at a loss.

Short Put

Similar to the long put, the short put strategy is where you sell a put with the expectation that the price will rise above the strike price by the end of the trading period. In this strategy, you receive cash as a premium for selling a put. If the stock is below the strike price by expiration, you will be forced to purchase the underlying asset at the strike price.

The strategy is also known as the naked or uncovered put and gives an investor the right to purchase shares of an underlying stock when a put option buyer exercises the option.

For you to initiate a put option using this strategy, you have to be sure that the cost of an underlying asset will remain above the striking price. If the option expires worthless, you risk losing part of your initial investment. One downside of this strategy is that the profit is limited by the premium received, and there is a significant amount of risk involved. You should, therefore, use it only when they are positive that the stock will go up. You must also ensure that there is enough equity in your account to purchase the underlying stock should the put options work against your expectations.

Bear Put Spread

This is one of the best strategies for beginners since it involves short put spreads. The bear put spread can easily be applied to small and new trading accounts. It does not have any restrictions in terms of shares or premiums. It is also known as the short put spread and involves the selling of puts.

You can use this strategy when expecting the stock to remain at the same value or increase in price until the expiration date. If this happens, the option will expire worthlessly, and you will get your whole premium back.

To set up the bear put spread, start by selling a put option, then purchase another put option with a lower strike price than the one you sold. The option you buy should have the same value and expiration date as the one you sold. This makes your sold put more expensive than the one you bought, translating into some profit.

Unlike the long call, which returns multiple times of the investment, the short put spread can only give you a maximum return that is equal to your initial premium. This amount will be determined by the direction of the market. If the stock remains at the same level or goes beyond the strike price, you will get your premium back. If the stock decreases below the strike price, you will be forced to purchase the underlying stock at the strike price, and this result in loss.

Investors use this vertical spread strategy to make a profit from selling premiums to other investors who have bet against the stock prices going up. Because put sellers often have a certain number of shares to their name, they cannot get stuck when it comes to paying out on losses. In case you need to use this strategy, you must be careful that you do not sell your puts without first understanding the market. This is because stock prices may fall and claim all your premiums.

Other strategies combine put and call options to maximize profits. Some of them include the following.

Protective Collar

The protective collar strategy comprises of an out-of-the-money put option and a call option that run concurrently. This strategy is not so common in beginners, but if you master it correctly, you can lock some good profits from it. The combination of call and put options allows you to have downside protection to your stock while enjoying potential profits on the upside. It is the same us running the covered call and protective put strategies at the same time.

Investors use this strategy as another option to stop orders since they have the right to choose when to exercise their options. You can implement this strategy with little or no cost since the premium you get from the short call can be used to cancel out the cost of the long put. The strategy is called a collar because it helps you limit both downside and upside risk.

Long Straddle

The long straddle allows you to buy a put and call option at the same strike price, stock value, and expiration date. It is used by traders who predict that the value of the stock may go beyond the normal range, yet they are unsure of the exact direction this will take. The result of this strategy is often an unlimited gain. The loss is often tied to the combined premiums of the two options that are the call and put.

Iron Condor

This strategy combines the bear call spread, and the bull put spread. It involves selling an out-of-the-money put and purchasing an out-of-the-money put at a lower strike price. You then sell an out-of-the-money call buy a call at higher strike prices. Al these options are initiated at the same expiration date and on the same stock value.

The iron condor strategy is mostly applied to low volatile stocks in order to earn a net premium from the options spread. The combination of put and call options makes this strategy non-directional, thus creating a possibility to make profits either on the upside or downside. You can apply it on short-term or long-term trades depending on the performance of the market. The higher the trading range, the higher the profits realized.

Most beginners are always eager to start trading that they forget to look for the appropriate knowledge and skills for success. These strategies give you an opportunity to maximize profits on your options trading account. It is essential that you take time and build a solid foundation that will increase your chances of succeeding in your trades. The idea is if you do not know what you are doing, you will definitely end up losing your money. With a good strategy, you can start making profits as soon as you start trading.

Chapter : 8
An Example of a Trade

Trading options is a lot more beneficial and profitable than trading in stocks. Additionally, trading options is much easier than what many people consider them to be. Let us look at an example of a trade.

Example

Imagine GRANK is currently trending at $80, and from your analysis, you feel the price will move to $100 in a few weeks to come.

One of the ways to make money from this is to acquire 200 shares of the stock at $80 then when the price hits $100; you sell it off. The decision will cost you $8,000 today, and you will then make $10,000 when you sell it off in a few weeks. This translates into $2,000 profit and a 25 percent profit margin.

Here is a breakdown of the whole process:

Type of trade	price	Sales proceeds ($100)	Profit
100 shares @ $80	($8,000)	$10,000	$2,000
1 share 40 call at $3	($300)	$2,000	$1,700
20 share 40 calls at $2	($4,000)	$20,000	$16,000

The good thing about options trading is that you can make huge profits in such a short time. This is only true when you understand the price movement within that short amount of time.

Let us break down the trade so that you understand what is happening:

Buying one call option contract (100 shares) of Grank with a price of $80, which expires in 3 months.

Let us assume the option was priced for $3 per share. This will cost $300 per contract because each option contract represents 100 shares. So, a price option of $3 means that the contract is trading at $300.

Buying a call option on Grank gives you the ability to trade 100 shares at $80 per share within the specified period, as long as it is before the date of expiration.

If the option goes to $100, the cost of selling the option goes to $20 for each contract, which means the strike price will go for a minimum of $20, which translates into $2000 per contract. This means the option has an intrinsic value of $20.

What Happens When Grank doesn't go up to $100 staying at $90?

If the price of the option rises above $80 by any value by the expiry date, then the call options are still viable with the difference of the current price minus the buying price. For instance, if it goes to $90, you can still make a profit of $10 per option when you sell them.

The good thing is that you don't have to sell off the shares immediately. You can still wait for the value to increase. You can hold on until the option reaches the price you desire.

What if the Price Stays around $80?

Now, what if the market price doesn't rise as you expected and just lingers around the original price till the expiry date. This means the option stays at the same price and will expire without making you any money. No one will be willing to buy the options at a price of more than $80 in the market. Here, you only lose the fee that you put up for the option.

What if the Price Falls Below $80?

Well, if the price falls below $80, remember you don't have an obligation tying you down to buying the option at any price – you simply do nothing just sit back and let the time run its course. You only lose the money that you put up for the option.

Key Takeaway

Always know that when you acquire an order at a certain price, you need to have someone that is willing to sell the option. You can engage in the options trading market as a buyer or a seller.

You also need to remember that options give you the ability to purchase the stock at a given price and then sell it before the expiry date. The call option requires you to call the stock away from a seller, and the put option requires you to sell the stock to someone.

Chapter : 9
Tips for Success

Options fall among the most flexible trading instruments on the financial market today. They allow traders to make money from the downside, upside, and sideways movement of the market. There has always been a myth that options trading is both risky and complicated. It is easy to see options as something difficult to trade in, but this is not true. Only that using options as a trading instrument involves several risks, just like any other instrument. Not everyone comes out successful. However, anyone with good basic information about options can successfully make it in the market.

Most successful traders have tips and tricks that they employ to ensure they make some good profit trading options. Here are some of them.

Understand Technical and Fundamental Analysis

Before you start trading, ensure that you carry out an analysis of the market. Technical analysis involves the study of how the price is expected to change. The idea behind this concept is that you can study historical patterns in price changes and determine how the price may change in the future.

Fundamental analysis, on the other hand, helps you to analyze social, economic, and political factors that may affect the demand and supply of the stock you wish to trade in. Supply and demand affect the price change and can be used to detect the direction of stock prices easily. In a nutshell, technical, and fundamental analysis of the market helps you to identify similar patterns around the price and make informed decisions on your options.

Have Enough Capital

The reason why most beginners do not make it in options trading is not having enough capital. Most people get excited at how easy options trading can be and think that they can make an instant profit from their little capital in a matter of days. However, before they realize it, a few trades have swallowed their capital. They are then left with nothing to trade on. To be on the safe side, start with a good amount of cash that can sustain you for a number of trades.

Get a Suitable Trading Style

What differentiates traders is their preferences, personalities, and trading styles. You need to understand the style that suits you best. For example, some traders prefer working at night, while others are more effective in day trading. Some of the traders will make several short sales during the day while others will factor in the issue of time and volatility just to gain a large profit over periods that may last between few days and a month.

Learn from your losses and use the information to make better trades in the future. You need a lot of time to practice on a trade before engaging in the real trade.

Back-test Your Trading Strategy

Back-testing is a very important aspect when it comes to developing a winning plan. It entails evaluating your existing strategy and style against the market history to see how best you will perform. Although past performance does not necessarily determine future success, doing this will give you a rough picture of how your strategy and style may perform at different times and setups. In case you are unable to do this by yourself, you may engage a software company or Forex broker to do the back-testing for you.

One advantage of back-testing is that it helps you identify areas within your strategy that need to be improved. For the process to be accurate, you need to consider a few factors, which include:

- *Ensure the time period is accurate.* It is recommended that you test a strategy over long periods of time than short ones. This is because long periods often produce good results.
- *Stick to one sector.* If your strategy is confined on options trading, then your back-test should only focus on options trading.
- *Do not use results to make conclusive decisions.* In most cases, past performances may not necessarily reflect what happens in the future. As much as back-testing may depict your strategy as an excellent one, it is good to leave room for possible failure or underperformance of the strategy

Create a Risk Management Plan

When it comes to options trading, do not invest any money that you are cannot afford to lose. Before sealing a contract, think about the worst-case scenario in terms of what you may lose from the transaction and if you will be able to endure the loss. Beginners always have a problem getting over a loss. To help you remain on the safe side, do not put large percentages of your capital in a single trade. Always split your capital into bits, spare some money in an interest generating account, then use the rest for trading. This ensures that you do not lose all your capital in options trading.

Having a plan is vital for your success. You need to have it in place before you start trading. Remember, options are high-risk tools, and it is important to have strategies in place that can help you minimize the risks involved with each trade. Use your money wisely. Diversify the stocks you trade in to reduce the potential of losing all your capital. Most of the expert traders only seal a contract when there are low risk and high profits.

Be Patient and Disciplined

To succeed in options trading, you must develop a high sense of discipline. Carry out extensive research and set the right goals. Stick to these goals and have them in mind as you seize trading opportunities. Be careful that you do not follow the crowd and don't believe in some facts and opinions before doing some research. In other words, have a strategy that is independent of external influences. This does not mean that you ignore forums that provide you with useful information about options trading and the financial market at large. Just be sure to study the trends, learn from the market, and make useful trades based on your findings.

Patience will help you get the right opportunity to make a profit. Expert traders can stay idle for days, just watching the market and waiting for a good time to make or close a sale. Impatient traders will always complain of less profit or huge losses. Wait for the odds to work in your favor and focus on the bigger picture.

Patience and discipline will help you stick to your capital and risk management plans. These attributes also assist you to avoid trades you are not successful in.

Understand the Market Cycle

The options trading market keeps changing every time. You need to remain updated on the market trends and make the necessary adjustments to your plan accordingly. Through constant learning, you will be able to learn new strategies and identify better trading opportunities that another traders bypass.

Understand when to trade and when to exit. Know when the market is taking an uptrend or declining. Follow and interpret

Forex news to understand what to expect in the future and where the industry is heading.

Keep Records

Having a record of your past trades can help you determine when to make a call or put option successfully. Some of the successful traders keep records of all their transactions. Analyzing these records continuously can help you identify vital patterns in the options you are trading in. It can also help improve your odds in the trade.

As you study the records, be sure to maintain some level of flexibility depending on your performance on each market. Learn how to exit a market that is not working in your favor. You must also accept any losses incurred since this forms part of every learning process. Options trading always deals with numbers so you must be good at making useful calculations.

Succeeding on Calls and Puts

As you may understand, there are several types of options trading, including call and put options. A call contract implies that the trader is expecting the price to go high and wants to make a profit from this increase. A put contract, on the other hand, means that the price is expected to decline, and a trader can realize a profit from this decline.

As you trade, you must be able to tell the direction of the stock to benefit from the call and put options easily. Beginners are always advised only to buy contracts to avoid the risk of using all the money set for the contract. Being a seller of an options contract puts you at a high risk of loss. Although your goal is to ensure that the option expires without you losing anything, you will need to part with an unlimited amount of stock if the prices go down. This leaves you with big liabilities.

Additionally, you must understand the difference between purchasing an option 'in the money' as opposed to doing this 'out of the money.' Purchasing an option in the money means that there is a value charged to your account in the options contract. This amount will be deducted from your account together with the contract price. Out of the money trading, on the other hand, is cheaper, but there has to be a change in the stock price before reaching the strike price for an option's value to be improved.

Mistakes to Avoid When Trading Options

At every level of options trading, there are mistakes that people do over and over again. However, these mistakes must be avoided in order to realize a profit from the trade. Some of the common mistakes you should avoid are:

Not Defining an Exit Strategy

Just like in stocks trading, you must be able to control your emotions when trading options. Once you have a trading plan, stick to it, and do not be quick to exit no matter how bad things become. To help you achieve this, define your upside and downside exit points in good time. You also need to define the timeframe for your exit, although the trade gives you an opportunity to get out of a call or put option before it expires.

Attempting to Recover Past Losses

A trade can move against you and make you lose money. Most traders have been there. Sometimes you may put your capital on options, and the outcome is not exactly what you expected. In such a scenario, most traders tend to double up their options strategy to see if they can recover the loss. Doubling may lower your potential for loss in a given trade, but it is surrounded by a lot of risks.

In most cases, it does not work. Most traders who try out this technique end up losing a lot more. Once a loss occurs, it is wise to close the trade and start a different trade to see if you can recover your money.

Trading in Illiquid Options

Liquidity in options trading refers to having active sellers and buyers on the market all the time. This is what drives competition. It also affects ask and bid prices for options and stocks. The stock market is often more liquid than the options market because stock traders focus on one commodity, while options traders often have several contracts to select from. An option quote always has the bid price and the asking price indicated on it. These prices do not indicate the actual value of the option. Illiquidity in options trading may result from illiquid stock. It is therefore important to trade options that are derived from a highly liquid stock.

Redeeming Short Strategies Too Late

Always ensure that you buy back your short strategies in good time. It is important not to assume that a trade will go your way the entire time. This is because trade can change performance in a matter of seconds. In case a short option gets out of the money, and you are able to redeem it then do so before you lose more money in the transaction. One rule of thumb that most traders use is that if you are able to keep 80% of your gain from a sale, then you should buy it back as soon as you can.

Do not allow yourself to learn the lessons the hard way. It is not always wise to attempt a trade while you already know the kind of risks involved. Focus on your trading plan and commit to these tips to succeed in your trade.

Chapter : 10
Conclusion

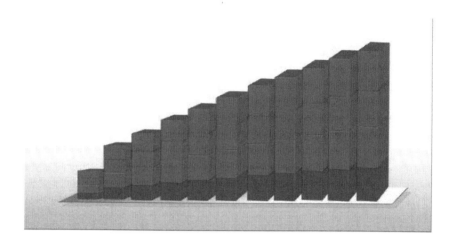

Options trading is such a unique yet valuable way of making money in the stock market. While there are some risks involved in the trade, these are normally limited, giving you a chance to make some good money from the trade. Adequate market research and knowing when to make a move will help you succeed in options trading. Brokers can also assist too since they can help you trade before you master the business.

After reading this book, you must have figured out how easy options trading is. With the information covered here plus your desire to make it in options trading, you have no option but to excel in the business. You are now better prepared to trade options using technical analysis, fundamental analysis, and other procedures. You are also ready to take opportunities as they come and have a sense of what each trade entails, from a technical view.

Trading in options is a process. The more prepared you are, the better the experience. Of course, the starting point lies in to understand what options trading is. Options are an alternative strategy for Forex investors who do not wish to trade in underlying securities. The basics involve understanding how to purchase and sell calls and puts. This is what constitutes an options contract. Let us recap a few points from this:

- An option refers to a contract that gives a buyer the authority to buy or sell an asset at a certain price within a certain period.
- Options do not represent the real value of an asset or underlying security. An option in itself is a derivative of an asset or security
- Calls give you the right to purchase an asset while puts allow you to sell an asset.
- The options market has four participants. These are the buyer of a call, the buyer of a put, the seller of a call and the seller of a put.
- The cost of an option is referred to as the premium.
- Long-term options are also known as leaps

With basic information at hand, you are now ready to attempt your first trade. How you embrace the strategies outlined in chapter 7 above determines how far you can go in options trading, especially if you are a beginner. The power of options lies in their versatility. However, this versatility comes with a cost. If not handled carefully, the trade becomes riskier than stock. That is why you will come across many disclaimers advising you to only engage in options trading using risk capital. This book plays a vital role in helping you appreciate the principle of decaying time and how it applies to options trading. Without understanding how this principle works, any trade that you carry out will be surrounded by diverse risks and uncertainties.

By now, you understand that there are a good number of tools and platforms that you can use to trade options. Since the cost of options keeps fluctuating from the start date to the maturity date, you need a platform that best suits your trading and training needs. Bear in mind that each platform has its strengths and weaknesses; therefore, you may not find one that is 100 percent effective. A good platform is one that gives you the ability to tailor your experience. Such a platform can accommodate both novice and experienced traders. A sophisticated platform can negatively impact your proficiency since you will spend a considerable amount of time trying to

Options Trading

understand the advanced tools and features on the platform. Having the right instrument will ensure that you trade with confidence.

Of course, we could not end the discussion without mentioning financial leverage as a benefit of trading options. The leverage comes about when you are able to translate your little capital into huge gains. It arises from the fact that a percentage increase in the price of an option is relatively higher than the increase in the underlying asset. This means that the more you invest, the higher the financial leverage. With a good trading plan, you can use this concept to minimize trading risks and maximize your returns. A great advantage in options trading is that the options contract itself is already a leverage opportunity. It allows you to grow your starting capital easily. By now, you should be able to calculate the leverage of any given position using the delta value.

While you can succeed in options trading without carrying out any technical analysis, it may be difficult for you to determine the duration, direction, and range of movement within the market. Since options are always subject to decay, any slight change in the values is very important. Understanding technical analysis indicators such as the RSI, IMI, and MFI can go a long way to ensure that you manage volatility, minimize risks, and close your trades with a profit.

As a trader, you must always choose an indicator that complements your trading strategy and style.

When it comes to options trading, patience and commitment are key. You must be able to control your emotions. Emotional trading is a risky affair. Treating options like any other business can help manage losses with ease. Making trades just because they seem good can lead you into trouble. Actually, the difference between good traders and average ones is that a good trader does not allow emotions to control him. When he loses, he understands that it is because he made a wrong move or choice and that it is not the system that is working against him. Good traders do not dive into unnecessary opportunities just because of feelings; they weight the options and make decisions based on what is in the trade for them. They also understand when to quit from trade even if some losses are incurred.

We also looked at some of the tips you need to employ to ensure that you succeed in most of your trades if not all. These are simple things such as collecting enough capital before you start trading, identifying a suitable trading style, and having a risk management plan. You also have known some of the mistakes most traders make when trading options and how you can avoid them.

With all this insight into the options market, you should be able to carry out a trade from start to finish, successfully. You must, however, note that the options business is not for every investor. It can get sophisticated and dangerous if you do not put the information outlined in this book into practice.

By now, it is clear to you whether this is an investment you want to try out or not. If you are into it, then you must decide the kind of trader you would want to be. You can either be a day trader, long term trader, or a short-term trader. As a day trader, you will have the advantage of making several trades that close quickly. This option is good for you if you are interested in making small profits. Otherwise, consider long-term trading that can span a period of over 30 days but with incredible profits.

Like stated earlier in the book, trading on options also involves choosing the underlying security that you would wish to connect your options to. This may be in the form of commodities, stock, or foreign currency. Each currency has its own characteristics, and the liquidity status also matters. Commodities are good but very volatile, currencies trade most of the time, but the prices are easily influenced by economic news items. Stocks experience a rapid change in prices overnight.

To many people, options are a complicated instrument to trade in. However, the more you learn about them, the simpler they become. With some experience, you realize that the instrument is one of the most flexible to trade in. Nonetheless, for options trading to go well, you also need to understand the basics of picking a stock, assessing market cycles and formulating investment strategies.

Since options are highly volatile, if you do not exercise caution, you may lose all your investment at one go. That is why you need specialized training such as this one before venturing into it. A good number of people that have succeeded in options trading began as stock traders. If you are already into stock trading, you will have easy time trading options due to the many similarities that exist between the two.

Lastly, it is important to note that the shorter the trading period, the higher the stress and risks involved. If you keep holding your trades through the night, you stand a high risk of losing all your capital and destroying your account. Other than this, we are glad that you have learned a new way of earning money from the financial market and understood all the traits and skills you need to make it in binary options trading. Note that theory is never effective without practice. So, in case you need to get started, it is best to identify a trading platform and put what you have learned into practice. Remember, the more you practice, the more confident you become.

Made in the USA
Middletown, DE
31 October 2019

77675944R00077